KWANZAA GETS AN A

Written by Steven C. Thedford

Illustrated by LaSquizzie Kern

NWP
New World Press, Inc.
Atlanta

For Kennedy I. Thedford,
a daughter who asked the questions that sparked the idea for this book.

Watoto (children) came to the library
to hear a story of Kwanzaa that they had
heard before.

Waiting boys and girls talked on the floor.

When the children saw the griot (storyteller)
walk through the door,
all the kids started to roar.

The griot entered the children's reading area
and looked around.

He smiled at the children in their little town.

The griot sat down,
dressed in an African gown.

"Do you want to hear how Kwanzaa got an A?" asked the griot.

"Yes!" screamed the watoto.

"That's very good," said the griot. "But not so loud."

The children nodded in agreement.

The griot laughed
and walked around the children.

"When I raise my walking stick,
please say 'Ashe [ah-**SHAY**].'
Can we practice?"

"Yes," replied the watoto.

The griot raised his walking stick.

"Ashe," said the watoto.

"One more time," said the griot.

The griot raised his walking stick.

"Ashe," said the watoto.

The griot began to speak in a mysterious way.

"In 1965 there was a riot in Watts, a
neighborhood in southern Los Angeles, on a
hot summer day.

African Americans in the community were
disrespected in that fray.

They wanted those who were hurting
their lives to pay.

Others turned to their faith,
fell to their knees, and began to pray."

The griot raised his walking stick: "Ashe."

Dr. Maulana Karenga, a teacher, wanted to restore the community destroyed by racist horseplay.

"Return to Africa!" was his cry. He researched our history to reduce the disarray.

Dr. Karenga believed the people needed to celebrate themselves the right way.

The griot raised his walking stick: "Ashe."

Dr. Karenga created a harvest festival similar to the Egyptian and Zulu, a cultural holiday.

He named it Kwanzaa after the Swahili phrase, *"matunda ya kwanza,"* a phrase we should repeat every day.

It means "first fruits (of the harvest)." It is a time to renew and remember so we won't stray.

The griot raised his walking stick: "Ashe."

The first Kwanzaa was held in 1966
in Los Angeles, California,
a city near Santa Monica Bay.

It started in a tiny apartment, and
celebrations were small back in the day.

Yet, Kwanzaa has come a long way,
and events are large today.

The griot raised his walking stick: "Ashe."

Portraits of great African Americans
hung on the walls, a sacred display.

Artifacts from the motherland adorned the
apartment to invite the ancestors to convey.

Kente cloth and other African fabrics were
everywhere on that day.

The griot raised his walking stick: "Ashe."

Dr. Karenga discussed the importance of the symbols of Kwanzaa during the entree.

The *kinara, mkeka, muhindi*—were special and new, which made it more than some tired cliché.

He challenged the people to a contest and rewarded the best a bouquet.

The griot raised his walking stick: "Ashe."

The children's program during the first Kwanzaa celebrated African countries like Zimbabwe.

Six watoto hung the holiday letters around their necks as entertainment at the African gourmet.

Dr. Karenga added an extra "A" to Kwanza so the seventh child at the event could participate at that moment in the USA.

The griot raised his walking stick: "Ashe."

The griot gestured for the children to
stand up, but stay.

Children on the floor stood in the walkway.

They put their fists into the air and pulled
them down seven times, halfway.

On the last one the watoto and the griot said,
"Harambee!"

GLOSSARY

Ashe (ah-**SHAY**): a West African philosophical concept through which the Yoruba of Nigeria conceive the power to make things happen and produce change.

Egyptians (ih-jip-shuh): an ethnic group native to Egypt; the citizens of that country share a common culture and a common dialect known as Egyptian Arabic.

Griot (gri-ot): a member of a class of traveling poets, musicians, and storytellers who maintain a tradition of oral history in parts of West Africa.

Harambee (hah-**RAHM**-bay): a Swahili word that means "Let's pull together."

Kinara (kee-**NAH**-rah): a candle holder that is a symbol of the ancestors of Africa.

Kwanzaa (**KWAHN**-zah): a week-long celebration held in the United States and in other nations of the African diaspora in the Americas. It lasts a week.

Mkeka (em-**KAY**-kah): a mat that serves as the foundation and should be placed before any other symbol on a Kwanzaa display.

Matunda Ya Kwanza (mah-**OON**-dah yah **KWAHN**-zah): "first fruits of the harvest."

Maulana Karenga: an African American professor of Africana studies, activist, and author. He is best known as the creator of the pan-African and African American holiday of Kwanzaa.

Muhindi (moo-**HEEN**-dee): an ear of corn that is a symbol of our children.

Swahili (Swa-**HEE**-Lee): a Bantu language widely used as a lingua franca in East Africa; Swahili is an official language in several countries.

Watoto: "children" in Swahili.

Zimbabwe (zim-**BAHB**-wey): a landlocked country in Southern Africa known for its dramatic landscape and diverse wildlife, much of it within parks, reserves, and safari areas.

Zulu (**ZOO**-loo): a member of a South African people who traditionally lived mainly in the KwaZulu-Natal Province.